to lead

STUDY GUIDE

Cover design by: Harper Creative
Cover photo by: Luke Edwards

ISBN: 978-1-960678-56-0   1 2 3 4 5 6 7 8 9 10

Printed in the United States of America

to lead

STUDY GUIDE

*A **Practical Guide** for Leaders in
Churches & Faith-Based Organizations*

Joel Milgate

AVAIL

CONTENTS

PART I: LEADING YOURSELF

PART II: LEADING OTHERS

to lead

A **Practical Guide** for Leaders in
Churches & Faith-Based Organizations

Joel Milgate

CHAPTER 1

TO LEAD IS GOOD

*To lead is to take
responsibility for a desired
future and influence
others to help create it.*

READING TIME

As you read Chapter 1: "To Lead Is Good" in *To Lead*, review, reflect on, and respond to the text by answering the following questions.

REFLECT AND TAKE ACTION:

Make a list of the people who led you during different stages of your life thus far and how their leadership accomplished good from which you are benefitting today.

_____

_____

_____

_____

_____

_____

In your own words, what is leadership, and how important is it?

_____

_____

_____

_____

_____

_____

Do you think anyone can be a leader? Why or why not?

_____

_____

_____

_____

_____

_____

What makes you unique? Write down at least three things.

_____

_____

_____

_____

_____

_____

What makes an effective leader? How are you an effective leader by this standard?

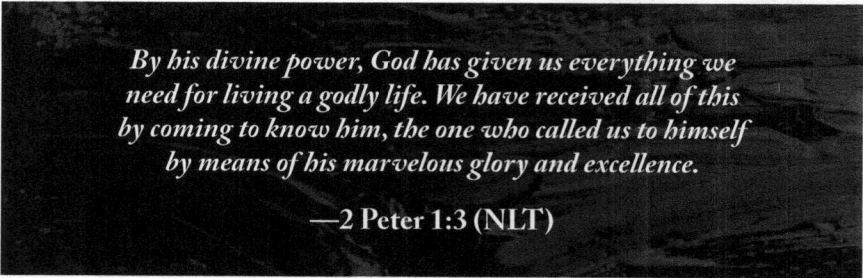

_____

_____

_____

_____

_____

_____

> *By his divine power, God has given us everything we need for living a godly life. We have received all of this by coming to know him, the one who called us to himself by means of his marvelous glory and excellence.*
>
> **—2 Peter 1:3 (NLT)**

Consider the scripture above and answer the following questions:

How does this verse encourage you in your life and leadership?

_____

_____

_____

_____

_____

_____

_____

Are you willing to say yes to the plans of God, even if they pull you away from your own? What might that look like?

_____

_____

_____

_____

_____

How are culture and leadership intertwined? What happens when a leader ignores the culture?

_____

_____

_____

_____

What kind of leadership did Jesus Christ exemplify? How do you demonstrate this kind of leadership?

_____

_____

_____

_____

_____

TO LEAD IS TO BE AN EXAMPLE

Being a great leader is more about presence than technique.

As you read
Chapter 2:
"To Lead Is to
Be an Example"
in *To Lead*,
review, reflect
on, and respond
to the text by
answering
the following
questions.

REFLECT AND TAKE ACTION:

What example are you setting for those you lead? What is your goal?

_____

_____

_____

_____

_____

_____

What intentional steps do you take to grow?

_____

_____

_____

_____

_____

_____

What does it mean to be an example of faith? Are you an example of faith?

_____

_____

_____

_____

_____

_____

> *You can identify them by their fruit, that is, by the way they act. Can you pick grapes from thornbushes, or figs from thistles? A good tree produces good fruit, and a bad tree produces bad fruit.*
>
> —Matthew 7:16-17 (ESV)

Consider the scripture above and answer the following questions:

How do you think the above verse pertains to your leadership?

_____

_____

_____

_____

_____

_____

_____

_____

What kind of fruit are you producing? Would those you lead say the same?

_____

_____

_____

_____

_____

_____

_____

_____

_____

What spiritual practices are a part of your daily routine?

_____

_____

_____

_____

_____

_____

_____

_____

_____

_____

_____

_____

What more can you do each day to draw nearer to God?

_____

_____

_____

_____

_____

_____

_____

_____

_____

_____

_____

_____

_____

TO LEAD IS TO PRAY

It doesn't matter in which spear you lead or how many people you lead; prayer matters, and it makes a difference. Always.

READING TIME

As you read Chapter 3: "To Lead Is to Pray" in *To Lead*, review, reflect on, and respond to the text by answering the following questions.

REFLECT AND TAKE ACTION:

What does your prayer life currently look like? How could it improve?

_____

_____

_____

_____

_____

_____

What is the importance of prayer? What is the reason you make time for prayer in your life?

_____

_____

_____

_____

_____

What are the different things that prayer does? Did any of the examples listed in this chapter surprise you?

_____

_____

_____

_____

_____

_____

Consider the scripture above and answer the following questions:

What do you think this verse reveals about prayer?

_____

_____

_____

_____

_____

_____

_____

_____

_____

_____

How often do you pray just to show gratitude to the Lord?

_____

_____

_____

_____

_____

_____

_____

_____

_____

Is there anything in your life that takes precedence over prayer? What is it? How can you change this?

_____

_____

_____

_____

_____

_____

_____

Which of the prayers listed at the end of this chapter do you need to pray?

_____

_____

_____

_____

_____

_____

_____

Take time to pray unto the Lord as many of the prayers as are applicable to you.

CHAPTER 4

TO LEAD IS TO GROW IN THE WORD

There is no need to reinvent the wheel; this wheel has served the church well and will continue to do so!

REFLECT AND TAKE ACTION:

How often do you get in the Word of God? Do you wish this was more often?

_____

_____

_____

_____

_____

_____

_____

In what ways is the Word of God important to our leadership?

_____

_____

_____

_____

_____

_____

What is the difference between understanding the Bible and being able to teach it? Do these come at the same time?

_____

_____

_____

_____

_____

_____

_____

> *Keep a close watch on how you live and on your teaching.*
> *Stay true to what is right for the sake of your own*
> *salvation and the salvation of those who hear you.*
>
> —*1 Timothy 4:16 (ESV)*

Consider the scripture above and answer the following questions:

What does this verse mean?

_____

_____

_____

_____

_____

_____

What does this verse reveal about our leadership and our focus in leadership?

_____

_____

_____

_____

_____

_____

What are the differences between theology and heresy? How do you prevent heresy from occurring?

_____

_____

_____

_____

_____

_____

_____

_____

What is orthodox theology? How do you encourage this in your organization?

_____

_____

_____

_____

_____

_____

Take time to study Psalm 1 by reading the Word. Use Bible study tools to get the full context and meaning of the passage.

TO LEAD IS TO TRUST

---

*Trust is the lifeblood
of relationships.*

READING TIME

As you read
Chapter 5:
"To Lead Is
to Trust" in
To Lead, reflect
on the questions
and scriptures.

REFLECT AND TAKE ACTION:

In your own words, define trust.

_____

_____

_____

_____

_____

On a scale of 1-10, how much do you feel
your team trusts you? Do you feel trusted?

1   2   3   4   5   6   7   8   9   10

_____

_____

_____

_____

_____

Are you a trustworthy leader? Why or why
not?

_____

_____

_____

_____

_____

_____

_____

_____

_____

How can you earn more trust from those who follow you? Are there improper ways to earn trust?

_____

_____

_____

_____

_____

_____

_____

Which of the different ways of earning trust listed in this chapter could you incorporate into your life and leadership?

_____

_____

_____

_____

_____

_____

_____

What does the saying "trust flows in several directions" imply?

_____

_____

_____

_____

_____

_____

How does trust in God help us trust those around us?

_____

_____

_____

_____

_____

_____

_____

_____

What crucial conversations do you need to have to rebuild trust with others?

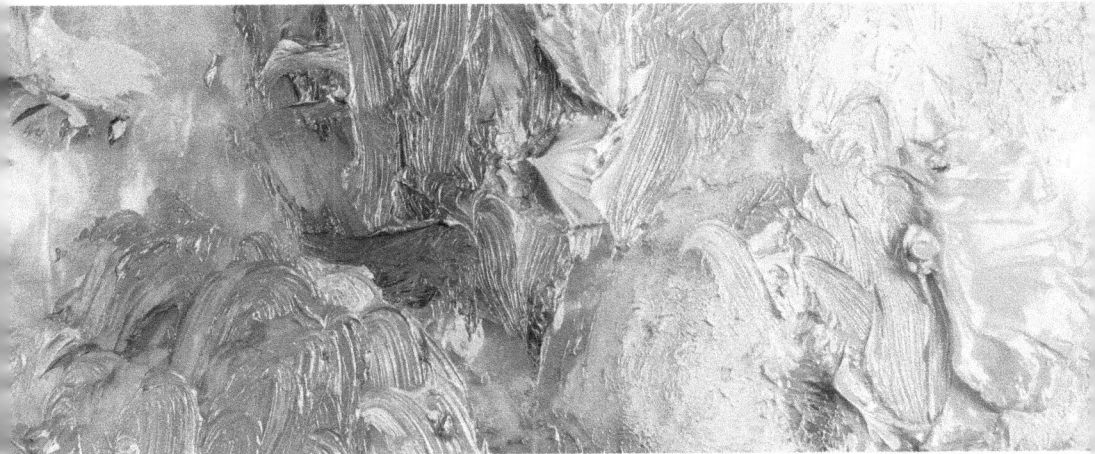

_____

_____

_____

_____

_____

_____

_____

_____

TO LEAD IS TO LEARN

———————

Leaders are learners.

REFLECT AND TAKE ACTION:

How are you investing in your growth as a leader?

_____

_____

_____

_____

_____

_____

Do you have a current learning goal or target? If so, what is it? If not, what might your goal look like?

_____

_____

_____

_____

_____

_____

Do you think humility is an important ingredient for learning and growth? Why or why not?

_____

_____

_____

_____

_____

_____

What good things can come from our demonstrating healthy humility?

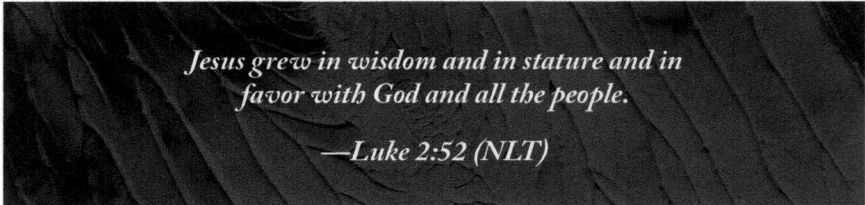

_____

_____

_____

_____

_____

_____

> *Jesus grew in wisdom and in stature and in favor with God and all the people.*
>
> —*Luke 2:52 (NLT)*

Consider the scripture above and answer the following questions:

Other than Jesus's physical growth, do you think the other areas of His growth happened intentionally or by default? Explain your answer.

_____

_____

_____

_____

_____

_____

Whom (if anyone) do you need to go to in order to seek forgiveness as you repent?

_____

_____

_____

_____

_____

_____

_____

Whom do you need to catch up with regularly and seek advice from?

_____

_____

_____

_____

_____

What do you need to be reading or learning in your current season?

_____

_____

_____

_____

_____

When was the last time you invited feedback from those around you?

_____

_____

_____

_____

_____

CHAPTER 7

TO LEAD IS TO OWN IT

_I can own it completely
but carry it lightly!_

REFLECT AND TAKE ACTION:

When have you had to "own it" as a leader? How did this make you feel?

_____

_____

_____

_____

_____

_____

Do you seek to stay in your comfort zone, or do you invite stretching and challenges? Why?

_____

_____

_____

_____

_____

_____

What are the differences between the hired hands and the shepherds talked about in John 10? Which are you?

_____

_____

_____

_____

_____

_____

_____

> *Never let loyalty and kindness leave you! Tie them around your neck as a reminder. Write them deep within your heart. Then you will find favor with both God and people, and you will earn a good reputation.*
>
> *—Proverbs 3:3–4 (NLT)*

Consider the scripture above and answer the following questions:

What jumps out to you from this scripture?

_____

_____

_____

_____

_____

_____

What do you think this verse means when it says the following: "Tie them around your neck as a reminder"?

_____

_____

_____

_____

_____

_____

Who has been entrusted to you? Write down as many names as apply. What do you feel as you look at this list?

_____

_____

_____

_____

_____

_____

What has been entrusted to you? How do you steward this
responsibly?

_____

_____

_____

_____

_____

_____

What tasks or assignments have you been entrusted with? Write
them down. What would it look like to fully own all of these tasks?

_____

_____

_____

_____

_____

Take time to read and pray the prayer provided at the end of this
chapter. What might God be speaking to you?

_____

_____

_____

_____

_____

_____

TO LEAD IS TO CARE

*People must come first—
before policy, before tasks,
and before everything.*

READING TIME

As you read Chapter 8: "To Lead Is to Care" in *To Lead*, reflect on the questions and scriptures.

REFLECT AND TAKE ACTION:

What do you put first in your organization: Results? Feelings? People?

_____

_____

_____

_____

_____

_____

_____

Do you feel leadership and love are intertwined? If so, how?

_____

_____

_____

_____

_____

_____

_____

How can you show the people you lead that you care? What are some practical ways?

_____

_____

_____

_____

_____

_____

_____

Of the ways to show people you care provided in this chapter, which do you need to work on most?

_____

_____

_____

_____

_____

_____

> *After breakfast Jesus asked Simon Peter, "Simon son of John, do you love me more than these?" "Yes, Lord," Peter replied, "you know I love you." "Then feed my lambs," Jesus told him.*
>
> —*John 21:15 (ESV)*

Consider the scripture above and answer the following questions:

Why do you think Jesus prefaced this command with a question about whether or not Simon Peter loved Him?

_____

_____

_____

_____

_____

_____

Why do you think Jesus chose to represent His children as "lambs"?

_____

_____

_____

_____

_____

_____

What is a "soul conversation"? How often do you have these with the people you lead?

_____

_____

_____

_____

_____

_____

When can you make time to sit down with someone in your care to talk, love them, ask questions, and show them you care?

_____

_____

_____

_____

_____

Take time to write out some questions (using the five listed at the end of this chapter as a starting point) that you will ask those you care about to guide the conversation.

_____

_____

_____

_____

_____

TO LEAD IS TO SERVE

We want people to know God in all of their lives and live their whole lives with a sense of purpose. That requires service.

READING
TIME

As you read
Chapter 9:
"To Lead Is
to Serve" in
To Lead, reflect
on the questions
and scriptures.

REFLECT AND TAKE ACTION:

What do you need to "take off" or "put on" in your leadership?

_____

_____

_____

_____

_____

_____

_____

In your current role, how can you serve the people you are leading?

_____

_____

_____

_____

_____

_____

_____

How can you be an example of a servant to those you lead?

_____

_____

_____

_____

_____

_____

_____

> *So he got up from the table, took off his robe, wrapped a towel around his waist, and poured water into a basin. Then he began to wash the disciples' feet, drying them with the towel he had around him.*
>
> *—John 13:4–5 (NLT)*

Consider the scripture above and answer the following questions:

What does this verse reveal about servant leadership?

_____

_____

_____

_____

_____

_____

What have you done to serve others through your leadership? Have you ever done anything on this level?

_____

_____

_____

_____

_____

_____

How can you motivate your team to serve others in a greater, more impactful way?

_____

_____

_____

_____

_____

_____

Make a list of the people in your realm of influence and write down one specific and practical way you can serve them.

_____

_____

_____

_____

_____

In what areas of life can you help the above individuals flourish?

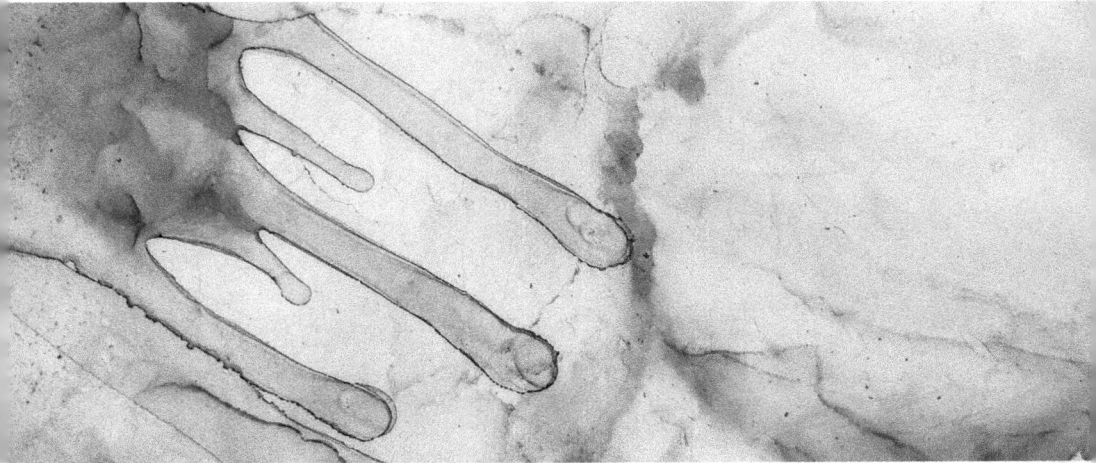

_____

_____

_____

_____

_____

CHAPTER 10

TO LEAD IS TO RECRUIT

The bigger the ask, the more intentional we need to be about how we recruit.

REFLECT AND TAKE ACTION:

When have you recruited someone you saw potential in to join your team? What was the result?

_____

_____

_____

_____

_____

_____

_____

How do you go about recruiting new talent?

_____

_____

_____

_____

_____

_____

_____

What is your vision? Do you communicate this vision when recruiting? Why or why not?

_____

_____

_____

_____

_____

_____

_____

> *I can't carry all these people by myself! The load is far too heavy! If this is how you intend to treat me, just go ahead and kill me. Do me a favor and spare this ministry!*
>
> *—Numbers 11:14-15 (NLT)*

Consider the scripture above and answer the following questions:

When have you ever felt something similar to what Moses was feeling in this passage?

_____

_____

_____

_____

_____

_____

_____

_____

Where do you think Moses went wrong? What was God's solution for Moses in Numbers 11:16-17?

_____

_____

_____

_____

_____

_____

_____

When recruiting someone, what are your nonnegotiables? Why have you selected these as your nonnegotiables?

_____

_____

_____

_____

_____

_____

_____

Whom do you want to recruit that you could set up a meeting with right now?

_____

_____

_____

_____

_____

_____

_____

_____

TO LEAD IS TO DEVELOP

---

*It's not about collecting people;
it's about developing people.*

READING TIME

As you read Chapter 11: "To Lead Is to Develop" in *To Lead*, reflect on the questions and scriptures.

REFLECT AND TAKE ACTION:

How do you develop talent within your organization?

_____

_____

_____

_____

_____

_____

What examples did Jesus set for us when discussing discipling leaders?

_____

_____

_____

_____

_____

_____

_____

Why do we have to develop others? What good things come when we intentionally develop others?

_____

_____

_____

_____

_____

_____

_____

Do you see any potential leadership qualities in the people you lead? Who are those people? What do you see?

_____

_____

_____

_____

_____

_____

_____

_____

How can we identify potential in future leaders?

_____

_____

_____

_____

_____

_____

Of the three stages of developing leaders (speaking vision, giving clarity, instilling confidence), which do you need to work on and why?

_____

_____

_____

_____

_____

_____

On a scale of 1 to 10, rate your team or group in the following three areas: hunger, humility, and honorable character.

HUNGER:

1   2   3   4   5   6   7   8   9   10

HUMILITY:

1   2   3   4   5   6   7   8   9   10

HONORABLE CHARACTER:

1   2   3   4   5   6   7   8   9   10

What conversations and experiences can you have together to intentionally develop those you lead?

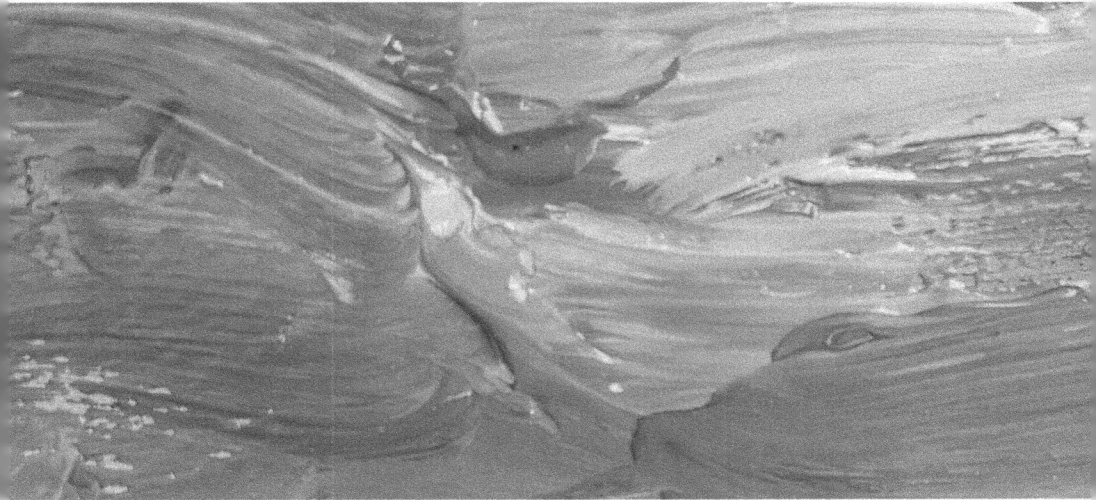

_____

_____

_____

_____

_____

_____

_____

CHAPTER 12

TO LEAD IS TO BUILD RELATIONSHIPS

Our primary mandate is to build relationships with people.

REFLECT AND TAKE ACTION:

In what way is building a relationship like building a bridge?

_____

_____

_____

_____

_____

_____

_____

_____

_____

_____

How often do you communicate with your team? Is your communication strictly business, or does it touch on personal matters as well?

_____

_____

_____

_____

_____

_____

_____

_____

_____

_____

What two or three individuals on your team are you closest to?
Why?

_____

_____

_____

_____

_____

_____

_____

Take time to devise a plan that will help you catch up (whether it be one-on-one or in a group setting) with everyone you lead. When will this plan start? How long will it take?

_____

_____

_____

_____

_____

_____

_____

Are you spending more time with some future leaders than others? Why or why not?

_____

_____

_____

_____

_____

_____

_____

What can you to develop a sense of family and fellowship with those you lead?

_____

_____

_____

_____

_____

_____

_____

_____

CHAPTER 13

TO LEAD IS TO HAVE VISION

---

*If everything's important,
then nothing's important.*

READING TIME

As you read Chapter 13: "To Lead Is to Have Vision" in *To Lead*, reflect on the questions and scriptures.

REFLECT AND TAKE ACTION:

In your own words, what is a vision? Why is it so important?

_____

_____

_____

_____

_____

_____

What is your church or organization's vision? What is your vision? Have you communicated this effectively to those you lead?

_____

_____

_____

_____

_____

_____

_____

Where did your vision come from? Has it changed over the years?

_____

_____

_____

_____

_____

> *Your word is a lamp to guide my feet*
> *and a light for my path.*
>
> *—Psalm 119:105 (NLT)*

Consider the scripture above and answer the following questions:

What do you think is the meaning of this scripture?

_____

_____

_____

_____

_____

How do you use God's Word in the same way for your life and leadership?

_____

_____

_____

_____

_____

How can your area or department contribute more to the bigger vision?

_____

_____

_____

_____

_____

What in your current role are you most passionate about? What causes you to pray?

_____

_____

_____

_____

_____

What do you think is possible to accomplish on and through your team with the Holy Spirit's intervention?

_____

_____

_____

_____

_____

How can you express vision in a way that is simple, repeatable, and memorable?

_____

_____

_____

_____

_____

TO LEAD IS TO SHAPE CULTURE

---

*You can't create a culture
around you that first isn't in you.*

READING TIME

As you read
Chapter 14:
"To Lead Is to
Shape Culture"
in *To Lead*,
reflect on the
questions and
scriptures.

REFLECT AND TAKE ACTION:

How would you describe the current culture of your organization?

_____

_____

_____

_____

_____

What is one negative aspect of your organization's culture? What is one positive, or your favorite, aspect?

_____

_____

_____

_____

_____

_____

How has your organization's culture changed over the past year? Over the past five years? Ten?

_____

_____

_____

_____

_____

_____

_____

_____

How does your organization's culture differ from kingdom culture?

_____

_____

_____

_____

_____

Do you think an organization's culture is a demonstration of its values? Why or why not?

_____

_____

_____

_____

_____

_____

_____

What stories need to be told? What heroes need to be celebrated?

_____

_____

_____

_____

_____

_____

What attitudes or behaviors in your organization need to be graciously confronted?

_____

_____

_____

_____

_____

What are the core values of your organization?

_____

_____

_____

_____

_____

What is your plan for shaping or adjusting your organization's culture? What needs to change, and what needs to stay the same?

_____

_____

_____

_____

_____

_____

_____